The ABCs of the Santa Spirit for Adults

The ABCs of the Santa Spirit for Adults

Yvonne Vissing

Vissing and Associates

CONTENTS

Dedication		1
1	Why The Santa Spirit?	2
2	A Brief History Of Santa Claus	7
3	A	26
4	B	30
5	C	33
6	D	36
7	E	39
8	F	42
9	G	45
10	H	48
11	I	50
12	J	53
13	K	56

14	L	58
15	M	61
16	N	64
17	O	67
18	P	69
19	Q	72
20	R	74
21	S	76
22	T	79
23	U	83
24	V	86
25	W	88
26	X	91
27	Y	92
28	Z	94
29	End Notes	96

Dedication

For Quixada, Chris & Leah

The ABCs of the Santa Spirit for Adults ©
Yvonne Vissing 2020
All rights reserved.
No content reproduction without the author consent.
Copyright information 2020 Yvonne Vissing
Paperback **ISBN 978-1-7358304-4-5**
E-book **ISBN 978-1-7358304-5-2**
First edition 2020
Publisher Information: Vissing and Associates LLC
Vissing & Associates, LLC. PO Box 273 Chester NH.
Email vissingandassociates@gmail.com

1

Why the Santa Spirit?

Santa Claus doesn't need just a face-lift or a make-over. He is long overdue for a major social transformation. We have the opportunity to use him today to teach children about important human values and behaviors such as altruism and gratitude. A writer's mantra is "show don't tell", and the Santa Claus figure provides a vehicle that does that. Children learn best when they have tangible examples of what we want them to learn, rather than from us lecturing them about it. Through the process of planning for Santa's arrival, we can show children what it means to think about others and how to find authentic happiness. We can use Santa as an example of joyful, loving-kindness that anyone and everyone can share.

Santa has become a problem for some people. Parents aren't sure if they should encourage their children to believe in him or not. What should you do when you want your child to experience visits from Santa but other children don't believe in him? How do you explain it to children when your children get presents from Santa but he doesn't come to some children's homes? Santa has become associated with materialism, not just of toys but of expensive items like computers, jewelry, and cars. Most families don't have the income or desire to have Santa bring those things. Santa comes at Christmas, a holiday associated with Christianity, so by default Santa has gotten linked with religion in some people's minds. He is usually depicted by being old, male, and white – and in a diverse society, those stereotypes are not necessarily symbols of inclusion. Then there is the age-old question – if you let your children believe in Santa, are you lying to them?

When adults ask the question, "Should I let children believe in Santa?" they want answers to support how to let their children enjoy the magic of believing in Santa Claus without the fear of lying to them. *The ABC's of the Santa Spirit for Adults* is designed to give adults an improved way of dealing with the Santa Claus issue, one that focuses on kindness and happiness. It will help anyone who interacts with children to enable children to have fun with the Santa character while putting his presence into a broader context that will help them to build bridges instead of conflict. It will help adults, whether you're around children or not, to rediscover the spirit of the holiday season inside yourself.

What is The Santa Spirit?

Helping children to believe in the **spirit** of Santa may be more beneficial to them than believing that he is a real person. Santa can be an action word, a verb, not just a noun; to Santa someone can mean to go out of your way to deliver happiness to others. The Santa Spirit embodies sharing and caring, and the attributes of goodness, altruism, and joy. It teaches children how to think about others, to prioritize what they really need and want, and how to make those things reality. The arrival of Santa teaches patience and the importance of using their imagination. Children need to play and be happy, and Santa provides us an annual opportunity to share joy with others. Giving, getting, and gratitude go hand-in-hand. The idea that Santa gifts all the children of the world because all children are special is a way to teach inclusivity and the appreciation of diversity. These are positive values for children to learn.

Santa Claus is real - at least, he is real in one form or another. He exists because he has provided immense value to children and adults across the generations. He can be found all around the world by different names and in one form or another. What is it about Santa that makes him so beloved? There are a variety of explanations. An obvious one is that he might bring us presents. Getting toys or sweets is something that children of all ages like. But sooner or later the sweets are eaten and the toys break. Despite this fact, children remember Santa warmly over time. Santa is not loved just because he brings sweets or treats on Christmas Eve. There's a bigger, better reason.

It's the process not the outcome, the journey not the destination, that often matters most in life. The weeks leading up to Santa's arrival can be filled with writing letters, making presents, decorating the house, baking cookies, singing songs, watching holiday movies together, and hearing stories from family members about days gone by. Family and friends we don't get to see often make time to visit and sometimes they bring us fancy wrapped presents to remind us that we're special. But the most fun is having them mingle around, snacking and chattering away, socializing children about what's important. We become a larger family, a community, at those moments. It warms our heart to feel that people care about us and that we matter to them.

The closer we get to the date of Santa's arrival, the more excited we get. Holding our breath with anticipation, we sneak out of our rooms early on Christmas morning to see if he actually came. We long to open our eyes to see if there is a cascade of colorfully wrapped presents under the tree. It is our fervent desire to know that all of the planning, work, and dreaming actually paid off. Believing in Santa Claus helps us to focuses upon our hopes about what we want and how we might make our dreams come true. He gives us an opportunity to build connections with our communities of families, friends, and neighbors. What we get materially isn't nearly as important as what we get emotionally from believing in Santa Claus.

It is the spirit of Santa that stays with us, year after year. It's the process of believing in Santa that's important, not necessarily what we get wrapped up from him. As the years go by, we tenderly caress the stocking secretly filled by loved ones for so many years. It warms us to remember whispering in bed beside our brothers and sisters to figure out if it really was reindeer hoofs we heard while we were supposed to be asleep. We grin as we remember certain holidays, like when the tree fell down after the cat decided to become a decoration in it or when Grandma dropped the turkey and the dog snatched it. We recall the ugly sweater, the dress that didn't fit, or the "what is it?" item we opened. Nodding to ourselves with grown wisdom, we come to appreciate how our parents never actually said Santa was real or imaginary. We respect how they managed to buy presents, hide them, and sneak them under the tree all without our knowing. And as we become older, we try to capture for our own children our dearest memories as we nibble the cookies they left out for Santa or stomp in the snow to make tiny reindeer hoofs.

In creating Santa for our children, we create Santa for ourselves. We embrace our own childhood memories and mingle them with dreams of what we hope our children might see as possible. For a predictable moment in time each year, we work to create a little magic for those we love. In doing so, we quietly make amends for times we were short-tempered, and when we didn't take the time to show them that we adore them with all our hearts. As adults, perhaps we need Santa Claus more than children do.

It's the spirit of Santa that we hold dear. Things come and go. But memories? They last forever. It's important to create happy memories in our children. As we grow we remember times when there was joy in the home and that people went out of their way to get us gifts because they loved us. If we were beloved then, perhaps we are beloved now. Dreams may become different, but dreams can still come true. In the pages that follow is a brief overview of the accurate history of Santa Claus followed by an A to Z primer on how to build the Santa Spirit.

2

A Brief History of Santa Claus

In order for you to wisely answer your children's questions about Santa, it's important for you to have a better idea about who he is and how he came to be. Most people don't actually know how Santa Claus came about.

Santa Claus is a universally beloved figure but he was never a real person. Rather, he has a history that is entwined with a variety of other characters, cultures, traditions, and stories. Understanding that is essential, because that means he didn't hail from any one particular person, country, religion, gender, or country. By his very origin, he was an inclusive, diverse figure. Common and desirable attributes were morphed into a central persona. As the years have gone by and advertisers – especially Coca Cola - got ahold of what he could deliver to him, he has become homogenized to look in a particular way. The reality is that a Santa Claus could look like anyone and everyone – it is the spirit or his altruistic, joyful persona that is key.

Across history, he has been known as King Frost, Pere Noel, Lord Snow, Winterman, Father Winter, Kris Kringle, Sinter Klaas or Sintirklass, Christkindlein, Kerstman, Papai Noel, Viejo Pascuero, Lam Khoong-Khoong, Santy, Dun Che Lao Ren, Old Man Christmas, San Nicolás, Ded Moroz, Shakhta Babah, Colacho, Hoteiosho, Samichlaus, Weihnachtsmann, Christmas Man, and Father Christmas. No matter what you call him, his essence is the similar, of a wise, elderly gift-bringer who brings joy and inspiration to the little people who will inherit the world. Santa's generosity is designed to help children to learn how to joyfully become good caretakers of each other.

One of the earliest Santa characters is Thor, a god of the peasants and common-folk in Nordic mythology. Unlike the Marvel comic and film character, Thor was depicted as an elderly man who was jovial, of heavy build, with a long white beard. His element was the fire, his color was red. He traveled by chariot, drawn through the sky by two white goats named Cracker and Gnasher. He lived in the "Northland" in a palace among icebergs. He was considered cheerful and friendly, never harming humans but helping and protecting them. The fireplace in every home was especially sacred to him, and he was said to come down through the chimney into the fire. At Yule, which is regarded as the calendar-year turning point when the earth moves from darkness to light, Thor would visit every home with a fireplace and bring gifts to children, who would put out their sabots, or wooden shoes, the night before. Good children received gifts of fruit, candy, and pieces of coal to burn in the fireplace so they could stay warm. Coal, therefore, was a good gift – not a bad one as children today are admonished to be good or "get a lump of coal in your stocking". It is interesting to note that in later years, Santa would sometimes be referred to as Christ of the Wheel (with the wheel being a pagan term for the calendar year). Notice the similarities - Thor, like Santa, dressed in red; Thor flew through the air on a chariot pulled by named goats while Santa flies through the sky in a sleigh pulled by reindeer.

Vikings traveled around the world, bringing with them their beliefs in the Northern deities and nature elementals. Their main god, Odin, came to earth dressed in a hooded cloak and listened to people and see if they were contented or not. Odin had a genial personality with the ability to cure diseases and predict the future. He carried a large satchel full of things to delight both the needy and the worthy. Odin was portrayed as a Sage with long flowing white beard and hair as he flew through the skies on his eight-legged white horse, Sleipnir. Eight is the number of transformation, and it is an interesting comparison that Santa's sleigh is typically pulled by eight reindeer. Odin, also known as Wodan (for which Wednesday or Wodan's day is named), was the god of wisdom and magic and his name means "the inspired one". He could travel to other worlds to gather more insight while his two black ravens Huginn (Thought) and Muninn (Memory) kept him informed about the news in the world. It is likely that Huginn and Muninn influenced the creation of elves, as did the nisse in Scandinavia.

But these are not the only historical figures that contributed to our perception of Santa Claus. By 600 AD when the Saxons had invaded and settled Britain, they brought along their celebration of spirits who were thought to bring the weather, such as King Frost or Lord Snow. It was customary for actors to dress up in costumes that represented those weather conditions. Pointed caps and capes were worn, draped with seasonal flowers such as holly or ivy. By encouraging these 'spirits' to join in the Saxton's feasts where there was extensive eating, drinking, and merry-making, it was hoped that the harsh weather would be kinder to them.

Father Winter came down from the northern mountains with the snows, dressed in furs and skins, heralding winter. This character was well known in Scandinavia, where Laps believed when he herded the reindeer down to lower pastures it was a sign that the winter snows were coming. Some allege that flying reindeer are actually manifestations of the god, Hermes. Father Winter had several other attributes that liken him to Thor. These include their relationship to fire - Father Winter's element was fire and he came through the fireplace. Laps had dome-shaped homes with one opening, which was both door and smoke hole, which would make it logical that Santa should enter the home through the chimney. They also shared the attribute of caring for others, since both Thor and Father Winter were thought to be benevolent protectors of the people and a lover of children.

In other parts of the world, such as in India and China, red-garbed hearth gods visited people's homes to keep them safe. Also, reverence for elderly men is woven into these cultures. Gifting as a symbolic message of honoring others is part of Asian culture. Even today, red is an important color and hearth-gods continue to be recognized as important.

While usually portrayed as male, the spirit of Santa may also be female. It has been found in mothers everywhere who seek to instill the joy of Christmas in their children, as well as historically in women such as La Bafana, who carried gifts in heavy bundles or baskets for long distances to deliver them to children. She is known to fly across the sky and enter through chimneys. The goddess Artemis was beautiful, generous, wise, and beloved whose companion animal was a deer, and is thought to be a contributor to our understanding of Santa Claus. St. Lucy displayed the spirit of Santa by leaving treats in children's shoes. As giving these women may have been, patriarchy took dominance so the Santa figure is almost always seen as male and elderly. Women were relegated to being domestic servants, baking cookies, and waiting on Santa, such as the example of Mrs. Claus (who interestingly doesn't even have a first name or her own identity).

As a recap, Santa is thus often associated with ancient societies, especially but not exclusively, in cold northern countries. Often he is associated where the hearth was common, where there may be hearth gods who came down the chimney to see if people had left offerings of food and drink for them. They were often clad in red (perhaps to represent fire), and would bless those who remembered them by leaving gifts of sweets, fun, or warmth. It was commonly thought that people who didn't do so would risk being cursed. Gifts were often carried in a bag by a friendly, caring, wise, magical older man who had a long white beard, dressed in a cloak, flew through the sky in vehicles pulled by animals and who may have little helpers.

Despite this varied history, some people associate Santa Claus with St. Nicholas. Hagios Nikolaos was born sometime around 280 A.D. in Patara, near Myra, in modern-day Turkey. His parents were devout Christians who raised their only child to practice faith through actions. His parents were reportedly quite wealthy, yet their money could not protect them from dying from an epidemic, most likely the plague. Orphaned young Haigos grew up in a monastery and became a priest at age 17, dedicating his life to faithful action. He gave away all the money he inherited from his parents as well as everything he owned. His generosity continued throughout his life. He had a fondness of helping children and the needy. People within the community and church were so touched by his kindness that he was rewarded by being made a bishop of his home-town. In keeping with the attire suitable to that position, Haigos wore the traditional bishop's pointed hat, or miter, and a long flowing white robe covered by a red cape. Like the men of his day, he did not cut his facial hair. Until 1300 AD, St. Nicholas was described to have a short dark beard, as would be common for a young Turkish bishop in those days. History indicates that he was not a jolly man but one who displayed angry, aggressive actions, such as destroying Artemis's temple or slapping heretics, for which he was imprisoned. He traveled the country by walking or riding in a horse-pulled wagon and was known to give money and other presents that he carried in a sack slung over his back. As was his custom, he chose to remain hidden while giving his gifts, so he often slipped into people's homes to deliver them while they slept. Haigos allegedly dropped little round bags of gold into stockings that poor, good children left by the fire to dry. Children who hoped that he would bless them with gifts were encouraged by their parents to go to sleep early since if they were awake they were concerned that he might not come. Because the golden bags were round and resemble oranges, it became customary for Santa to put oranges into the toe of children's stockings on Christmas Eve as a sign of good fortune.

He was called St. Nicholas after his death. He evidently had a good public-relations team that promoted his transformation as the predominant Christmas gift-giver. In the year 1119, a monk named Jean wrote the first known history of St. Nicholas; nuns in Belgium and France left candy in the shoes of children on his December 6 Feast Day, which is now known as St. Nicholas Day. The early Christian church didn't observe Christmas since it was associated with the pagan gods' feast days - the word "Cristes Maesse," or Christmas, didn't emerge until 1038. Long-dead St. Nicholas became so popular that in 1150 AD, Guace, a French scribe to the royal household, wrote the life of Nicholas as metric poems as sermons. Hilarius, who studied under Peter Abelard, wrote the first musical play about Nicholas in 1200, and over 500 songs and hymns had been written in honor of Nicholas by 1400. Over time his name was changed from "Saint" to "Santa," and from Nicholas to Klaus which later became Claus.

By the time of the Renaissance, St. Nicholas had become the most popular saint in Europe. But religious tensions of the day led to concerns about the devotion that should be given to saints, especially after the Protestant Reformation, when the veneration of saints began to be discouraged. By the 1500s people in England became less focused on St. Nicholas and favored Father Christmas. In Britain, each parish would employ a man from outside the parish to dress in long hooded disguised as Father Christmas to go to each home leaving a small gift. They took back to the priests any important news they had learned of the plight of the needy who needed help (similar to Huggin and Muggin, perhaps). From the 17th - 19th-century country mummers put on annual plays with Father Christmas, thereby keeping the gift-bearing visitor alive, even if more pagan than religious, as was the spirit of the times. It is interesting to notice that in the Macy's Thanksgiving Day Parade in New York City, the annual kick-off to the Christmas season, a mummer troupe always performs.

Why do all these Santa figures come around the winter solstice time? Gifting children on the date of December 25 coincides with the date of the winter pagan Brumalia festival in Rome. It was preceded by the Saturnalia festival that ran a week before, usually from December 17 to 24, which honored the winter solstice, or the day the sun begins its return to northern skies. The Saturnalia and Brumalia festivals were so popular that Emperor Constantine incorporated their festivities into those of the Roman Catholic Church. The Taoist festival Ta Chiu falls on Dec.27, which made merging traditional Taoist celebrations with those of others that fell around Dec. 25. December 25th was also a celebration day among the sun-worshippers of Mithraism, who regarded it as "the birthday of the invincible sun." Tammuz, the Babylonian pagan sun deity, was also celebrated during the solstice. Some religious scholars allege that the Christian cross symbol is actually the letter " t " the symbol for the pagan god Tammuz, thus the cross itself may be of pagan origin and date thousands of years before the birth of Jesus, which was likely not on December 25, but more likely in spring or in late September-early October during the Feast of Tabernacles. The actual date of the birth of Jesus is unknown. The December 25th date was selected as one of convenience because it merged together with the convergence of other festivals worldwide.

Santa could show up to deliver presents to good little girls and boys any time during Advent, from December 6 (St. Nicholas Day) to January 6 (Epiphany or El Dio de Los Reyes, the Festival of the Three Wise Men). Santa could arrive on Christmas Eve (December 24), on December 25, New Year's Day, St. Basil's Day, Boxing Day, St. Stephen's Day, or any time during the holiday season, which could range anywhere from a day to six weeks.

The major change of Santa Claus into a cultural icon occurred in the United States during the early 1800s. Prior to that time, the church during the 1600s, made it illegal for the Puritans to mention St. Nicolas' name. People were not allowed to exchange gifts, light a candle, or sing Christmas carols. Christmas was regarded as a totally religious, not secular, experience. But others felt it was God wanted people to celebrate, sing, dance, feast, and give gifts. This religious tension about the nature of God and how he wanted people to behave is longstanding. It is no surprise that people continue to disagree about the issues of God, Santa, and the role of this annual time of celebration, transformation, and gift-giving.

In an accidental twist of fate, Santa's popularity was increased in New York City during the melting pot era of immigration. In 1626, a fleet of ships, led by the Goede Vrowe (Goodwife), left Holland for the New World. The Goede Vrowe's masthead was St. Nicholas. The Dutch purchased some land from the Iroquois, for $24, named the village New Amsterdam and erected a statue in the square to St. Nicholas. That village was renamed overtime as New York. When Washington Irving, a member of the New York Historical Society saw a woodcut of a bearded man in the 1810 building, he incorporated that image incorporated into his writings. Writing under the pseudonym Diedrich Knickerbocker, Irving included describes St. Nicolas riding into town on a horse in his book *A History of New York*. Two years later he revised the book to show Nicholas riding over the trees in a wagon. This image undoubtedly influenced William Gilly who wrote an 1821 poem about "Santeclaus" who was dressed in fur and drove a sleigh drawn by a single reindeer as he delivered gifts. Gilly reportedly wrote this poem after he announced he actually observed Santa and his flying reindeer.

New Yorker Clement Moore is credited for creating the famous poem, best known as *The Night Before Christmas*. However, it is unclear that Moore really wrote the poem. Foster in his book, "*Author Unknown*," argues that "*A Visit From St. Nicholas*," was first published anonymously in a Troy, N.Y. newspaper in 1823 and it closely matches the verse of Henry Livingston Jr., a gentleman-poet of Dutch descent. Livingston, who lived in Poughkeepsie, N.Y. died before Moore was named as the poem's author. Whoever actually wrote it, the poem filled people's heads with images about what Santa may look like and how he may behave. Here is the now-famous poem that has forever colored our perceptions of Santa Claus:

The Night Before Christmas

Twas the night before Christmas, when all through the house Not a creature was stirring, not even a mouse.
The stockings were hung by the chimney with care,

In hopes that St Nicholas soon would be there.

The children were nestled all snug in their beds,
While visions of sugar-plums danced in their heads.
And mamma in her 'kerchief, and I in my cap,
Had just settled our brains for a long winter's nap.

When out on the lawn there arose such a clatter,
I sprang from the bed to see what was the matter.
Away to the window I flew like a flash,
Tore open the shutters and threw up the sash.

The moon on the breast of the new-fallen snow
Gave the luster of mid-day to objects below.
When, what to my wondering eyes should appear,
But a miniature sleigh, and eight tinny reindeer.

With a little old driver, so lively and quick,
I knew in a moment it must be St Nick.
More rapid than eagles his coursers they came,
And he whistled, and shouted, and called them by name!

"Now Dasher! now, Dancer! now, Prancer and Vixen!
On, Comet! On, Cupid! on, on Donner and Blitzen!
To the top of the porch! to the top of the wall!
Now dash away! Dash away! Dash away all!"

As dry leaves that before the wild hurricane fly,
When they meet with an obstacle, mount to the sky.
So up to the house-top the coursers they flew,

With the sleigh full of Toys, and St Nicholas too.

And then, in a twinkling, I heard on the roof
The prancing and pawing of each little hoof.
As I drew in my head, and was turning around,
Down the chimney St Nicholas came with a bound.

He was dressed all in fur, from his head to his foot,
And his clothes were all tarnished with ashes and soot.
A bundle of Toys he had flung on his back,
And he looked like a peddler, just opening his pack.

His eyes-how they twinkled! his dimples how merry!
His cheeks were like roses, his nose like a cherry!
His droll little mouth was drawn up like a bow,
And the beard of his chin was as white as the snow.

The stump of a pipe he held tight in his teeth,
And the smoke it encircled his head like a wreath.
He had a broad face and a little round belly,
That shook when he laughed, like a bowlful of jelly!

He was chubby and plump, a right jolly old elf,
And I laughed when I saw him, in spite of myself!
A wink of his eye and a twist of his head,
Soon gave me to know I had nothing to dread.

He spoke not a word, but went straight to his work,
And filled all the stockings, then turned with a jerk.
And laying his finger aside of his nose,

And giving a nod, up the chimney he rose!

He sprang to his sleigh, to his team gave a whistle,
And away they all flew like the down of a thistle.
But I heard him exclaim, 'ere he drove out of sight,
"Happy Christmas to all, and to all a good-night!"

Soon the combined image of St. Nicholas, the elf-like gift-bringer described by Moore, the amalgam of Kriss Kringle and pagan solstice figures morphed into the American collective mind. A man-sized version of Santa became the dominant image around 1841 when Philadelphia merchant J.W. Parkinson hired a man to dress in "Criscringle" clothing and climb the chimney outside his shop in order to encourage shoppers to visit his store. In 1863, a caricaturist for *Harper's Weekly* named Thomas Nast developed his own image of Santa as a figure with a flowing set of whiskers dressed in fur from head to toe. By 1866 his drawing of "Santa Claus and His Works" established Santa as a *maker* of toys. Three years later a book of the same name combined Nast drawings with a George Webster poem that identified the North Pole as Santa's home.

Until then, there was no consistent image of how big Santa was supposed to be. Sometimes he was described as large, tall, chubby, normal-size, slight-build, or small and elf-like. His clothing varied, from being dressed in furs or in cloth suits of red, blue, white, pink, gold, green, or purple. He was described as everything from a rascal with a blue three-cornered hat, red waistcoat, and yellow stockings to a man wearing a broad-brimmed hat and a huge pair of Flemish trunk hose. His countenance was often serious more often than jolly, though laughing Santa eventually became dominant. Boston printer, Louis Prang, introduced the English custom of Christmas cards to America, and in 1885 he issued a card featuring a red-suited Santa that was similar to Nast's 1881 drawing of "Merry Old Santa Claus." The chubby Santa with a red fur-trimmed suit began to become the dominant image of Santa Claus.

By the turn of the 20th century, Santa Claus had firmly established his place in American culture. However, the question of "is there really a Santa?" has always been present in the collective mind. The most predominant example of this is the 1897 letter that eight-year-old Virginia O'Hanlon wrote to the New York Sun. She had reportedly asked her father if there was a Santa, and her father (undoubtedly hedging the issue), encouraged the child to write to the newspaper, which was obliged only to state the truth. The newspaper's editor, Francis P. Church, wrote an editorial to the child in the paper – an editorial that has now become famous. It is as follows:

Yes, Virginia, There is a Santa Claus
Virginia O'Hanlon asked the paper:

I am 8 years old. Some of my little friends say there is no Santa Claus. Papa says, "If you see it in The Sun, it's so." Please tell me the truth, is there a Santa Claus?

Francis Church responded with this now-famous answer:

Virginia, your little friends are wrong. They have been affected by the skepticism of a skeptical age. They do not believe except what they see. They think that nothing can be which is not comprehensible by their little minds. All minds, Virginia, whether they be men's or children's, are little. In this great universe of ours, man is a mere insect, an ant, in his intellect as compared with the boundless world about him, as measured by the intelligence capable of grasping the whole of truth and knowledge.

Yes, Virginia, there is a Santa Claus.

He exists as certainly as love and generosity and devotion exist, and you know that they abound and give to your life its highest beauty and joy. Alas! how dreary would be the world if there were no Santa Claus! It would be as dreary as if there were no Virginias. There would be no childlike faith then, no poetry, no romance to make tolerable this existence. We should have no enjoyment, except in sense and sight. The external light with which childhood fills the world would be extinguished.

Not believe in Santa Claus! You might as well not believe in fairies. You might get your papa to hire men to watch in all the chimneys on Christmas eve to catch Santa Claus, but even if you did not see Santa Claus coming down, what would that prove? Nobody sees Santa Claus, but that is no sign that there is no Santa Claus. The most real things in the world are those that neither children nor men can see. Did you ever see fairies dancing on the lawn? Of course not, but that's no proof that they are not there. Nobody can conceive or imagine all the wonders there are unseen and unseeable in the world.

You tear apart the baby's rattle and see what makes the noise inside, but there is a veil covering the unseen world which not the strongest man, nor even the united strength of all the strongest men that ever lived could tear apart. Only faith, poetry, love, ro-

mance, can push aside that curtain and view and picture the supernal beauty and glory beyond. Is it all real? Ah, Virginia, in all this world there is nothing else real and abiding.

By the 1920s, there had been ingrained in our brains a socially accepted picture of what Santa Claus looked like. This image was seized upon by merchants for advertising purposes. Norman Rockwell created a Santa Claus that combined attributes of both the saintly and jolly when he created a picture for the Saturday Evening Post in 1922. From 1931 to 1964, Haddon Sundblom created Santa pictures for Coca-Cola advertisements that appeared world-wide on the back covers of Post and National Geographic magazines. The Coca-Cola image is the one that most people associate with Santa – a large, jolly-looking man wearing a red suit trimmed with white fur, leather boots and belt, long white beard, and a pack of toys slung onto his back.

While the benevolent "jolly old elf" is still around, media in the 21st century portrays Santa Claus quite differently from that of that when the 20th century dawned. Since the 1960s when the Coca-Cola Santa became pervasive, there have been new images of Santa introduced, and increasing amounts of Santa imagery. They include people of all ages, genders, races, and ethnicities. Today countries on every continent celebrate Santa in their own way, and parents have found ways to present him that are culturally specific, whether he wears warm furs, a cool red silk suit, or a red bathing suit! There are Santa runs, conventions, Santa Cons, and events where everyone dresses up as a Santa. Stores have begun putting out Santa merchandise before Halloween. Santa is still the giver of gifts on Christmas

Eve – although he has been known to come early or later to accommodate the complex schedules of today's families. Children may find that Santa visits them at the home of each grandparent, as well as the homes of mommy and daddy if the parents do not live together.

Because Santa Claus has been modified to fit the different cultures, climates, family, and community configurations, questioning the existence of Santa is now socially acceptable. There is a tendency for Santa to not be regarded as believable by any except the youngest of children. The time at which children begin disbelieving seems to occur much earlier now, with even very young children announcing matter-of-factly that there is no Santa. The classic film, The Miracle on 34th Street, was not the first public questioning of whether Santa existed, or whether anyone who believed in him might actually be crazy. A book published in London in 1678, *The Examination and Tryal of Old Father Christmas and his clearing by Jury*, was the first public analysis of whether Santa existed. The verdict in both – Santa does exist!

Santaologists around the world provide fascinating documentation of reindeer that can fly and the existence of elves such as in Robert Sullivan's book *The Flight of the Reindeer*. According to Swedish engineering consulting firm SWECO, the most logical place for Santa to live is not the North Pole but the Central Asian country of Kyrgyzstan, near the border with Kazakhstan. They calculated that if Santa's headquarters was there, he could reach every home on the globe from that location in 48 hours - providing his sleigh can maintain an average speed of about 21 million kilometers per hour and that each stop takes no more than 34 microseconds (a microsecond is one-millionth of a second). Scientific explorers allege that they have actually found where he lives, but some Santa scholars say the proof is in the Arctic, while others have been documented which house he lived in Turkey.

Santa may arrive on rooftops by reindeer or kangaroo pulled sleigh or come by plane, helicopter, boat or truck. He may slip down chimneys, leave treats in shoes, stockings, under trees, at the door, or on the table. His details are different from one place to another. But everywhere, there is a well-constructed explanation for why it is important to believe in Santa, even if believing is just for fun. Santa is just as important to children in the space age as he was when knights in shining armor rode on magnificent steeds when Vikings set out on amazing quests in hand-hewn boats, or as settlers ventured forth into the unknown in their Conestoga wagons.

Santa Claus has always been a figure of transformation. He will continue to transform as he changes and adapts to meet the demands of new time periods and social challenges. He fulfills a need that resides in children of all ages everywhere – we need to know we are beloved, that we matter, that someone cares and that someone appreciates the good things that we do. Transforming the Santa Spirit to be something delivered by people of any gender, any race, any age can help children see inclusivity, diversity, and how everyone in the community can influence other people's happiness.

In the pages that follow, you will find plenty of good reasons to keep Santa alive in your hearts and homes. He brings joy – and in these days, having the opportunity for joy, love, and building closer relationships may be something that we all need. After weighing all the pros and cons, this book is designed to give you A to Z reasons to feel more comfortable about how you let children believe in Santa Claus to find the Santa Spirit in their own heart. And guess what? As you read through the alphabet, you will likely rediscover the Santa Spirit in your own heart as well. The sharing of the Santa Spirit begins with YOU.

3

A

Anticipation, Awe, Altruism, Abundance, Affirmation

When we receive the thing we most hoped for, or are gifted with something wonderful we didn't expect, we get to experience a sense of awe. How did Santa know what would please us and how did he make it happen? Santa is designed to deliver things to children that they need or want, asking nothing for himself in return. In doing so, this reinforces altruism, or whole-hearted giving to others. Learning to be altruistic, thinking about how to help others, and finding joy in the process of doing so, is a valuable thing for children to learn. When Santa delivers gifts to all the children, there is a sense of abundance and an affirmation that everyone matters. The sharing of gifts, tables piled high with delicious foods, stockings that overflow and homes filled with exude music, glittery decorations, and sharing of good cheer affirms abundance and awe.

During much of the year children hear the messages, "don't

be greedy", "we can't afford that", "don't take so much", "you don't really need that" or "there's not enough to go around." Most of the time, parents don't mean to deliver harsh messages of lack. Rather, by saying such things we think we are teaching the children self-control, personal discipline, and the importance of waiting and sharing. Indeed, these are good lessons for children to learn. But such messages may also convey a sense of scarcity, insufficiency, of lack – not abundance.

Santa delivers the message of abundance. His round little belly shows he has enough to eat. He has more joy than he can contain, which escapes in easy laughs and jolly shouts of "ho ho ho!" He must have plenty of love in his heart for all children since his sleigh is piled to overflowing with toys and gifts for everyone. He has time to listen to what children dream about and to read their letters. He has countless elf friends working to make toys he can deliver. Santa supposedly gives all children something that they want or need, since inside everyone is goodness (even in those of us who have been a little naughty!). On Christmas morning when lucky children race down to see if "he came!", they stop and share a collective breath as they gaze upon bulging stockings and a mountain of presents. Of course, not all the gifts are for them – there are gifts there for everyone. Santa's arrival provides children an opportunity to see that there is a sense of plenty, and there is "enough" for each person. Symbolically, there is also the message that they too "are enough". Learning to look at the world as a happy and plentiful place helps to lay a foundation that could serve children well in the long run.

Anticipating what kind of cookie Santa would prefer helps children to think about what others would like. By wondering what Santa is doing in his workshop or as he prepares reindeer for the long journey ahead, children learn to put themselves into another's boots and view the world from his point of view. Children can barely sleep on Christmas Eve because they are so eager to catch Santa in the act of delivering them the things they have dreamed about receiving. Without the joyful anticipation of Santa, his arrival and the receiving of gifts would be much less magical and much more materialistic. Receiving gifts without the opportunity to dream, hope, and wish to make a gift, well, just a thing. One of the best gifts from Santa Claus is the chance it gives children to imagine that there is someone behind the scenes, working hard on their behalf, who is thinking about them and who is working hard to give them something that will make them extremely happy when the time is right. It isn't the material object that is the present – it is the thinking about the gift and all that it entails that is the most fun. Thinking about the pleasure one will receive from something that we make for them is satisfying and long-lasting.

Anticipating the arrival of Santa also teaches children to plan for something, learn time management skills, and how to think ahead. Just as Santa and his elves are hard at work for months before the big day, children learn that there is a deadline so they too must plan, save their money, go shopping, make or wrap their items. Advent or Christmas Countdown Calendars are very helpful devices for children to learn that there is a schedule that must be kept. It also helps them to tangibly understand that Christmas will come eventually, even if they have to wait longer than they might like.

On Christmas morning, after all the gifts have been opened, children have been known to ask, "is it over?" or "is that all?"

While these comments sometimes give their parents chagrin when they perceive greed, children are usually just asking for information for closure. They have been anticipating this moment for a long time. Asking questions about "are we done opening gifts" can simply mean, "can we go play with our toys now?" They may want to know if they can now run to the bathroom or get something to eat.

In dreaming about our first kiss, a wedding day, the birth of a baby, or the magic of Christmas morning, we all share in the common experience of lovely anticipation. The kiss may be wet and sloppy, the wedding day may be rainy, the new baby could have colic, and the Christmas gift may be the wrong size. But in the mental world of anticipation, there is the hope that everything will be just perfect. And you know what? Sometimes it is!

4

B

Benefits of Belief

Believing that Santa is real has benefits far beyond his bringing presents. Belief in him is a symbolic act that inspires children to think beyond the confines of everyday existence. On the surface, the Santa figure provides tangible things that children can wrap their heads around, like can reindeer really fly? Will he actually come? How does he know what I need and want? But belief in Santa gives children much more, things that could serve them well for a lifetime. Some are:

- Someone cares about me.
- The knowledge that someone is listening to me and working on my behalf that I may not even know.
- Believing that all children are important and matter since Santa can come to children everywhere.

- Having fun and playing is good for people and makes us feel happy.
- Being treated like I am special helps me to remember that I am. There is only one me and someone loves me just the way I am.
- Even when things look gloomy, predictable holidays remind us that there is always something wonderful to look forward to.
- Seeing that if you work hard as Santa does, you can make dreams come true.
- When you believe, the impossible could be possible.

The Santa character gives young children something they can comprehend that sets the stage for higher-order thinking later on. He can help us believe there is goodness aplenty in the world and many people who care about us. He can be used to demonstrate that even we don't know it, people exist who are working to do things for us, provide us things we need and want, and spend their time and energy making our lives better. We may never see them, but they exist nonetheless. Santa is not a god but belief in him helps lay a foundation for children to believe in a god, however one defines god to be, as children grow up.

Believing there is goodness in others we don't know helps us trust that others who are different from us, who live far from us or who look different from us may be nice too. He is an example of a global citizen that children can understand. The view that Santa comes to children everywhere coveys that all children are the same even when they are different, and everyone is special and important. Such a belief system is useful in children to appreciate the things that make us the same. It implies that diversity is normal and natural. This fosters a view that can be helpful in healing today's fragmented world.

Belief inspires us to think beyond what we can see, to expand our minds to see the world differently. There is an old saying that for those who believe, no proof is necessary - for those who don't believe, no proof enough is ever possible. When you believe, doors open wide where there were none before. When you don't believe, doors may close. When you believe something, you can make things happen that others would shrug off as implausible and impossible. Like the train in the story, *The Little Engine That Could*, believing that "I think I can" is foundational to expanding children's horizons to make things possible.

Belief in goodness, love, and joy gives our lives meaning. For believers, there are countless and obvious "facts" that prove Santa exists. If you aren't convinced that Santa could be real, look inside your heart and answer these questions: Do you love someone? Does someone love you? Can you "prove" that love exists? Even though love is invisible, you know when it exists. Love, like Santa, exists when you believe and act upon that belief. All we have to do is open our hearts and minds to find it.

5

C

Cheerfulness, Celebrations, Crafts, Caring, Cherish

Santa is always cheerful. His ability to be joyful while working hard is an attribute children are wise to emulate. Nobody likes being around grumpy people and sour-pusses. Cheer is something good to learn. Many parents get so engrossed with details to make a holiday "perfect" that they forget that being cheerful is more important than having the right table setting or prettiest wrapping paper. Children copy behaviors and attitudes that adults model as appropriate. Cheerfulness is an important deliverable during holiday celebrations.

Celebrations vary and no two families celebrate the same way. Everyone has their own traditions and memories that they seek to recreate in how they craft the holiday. The construction of Santa's wintertime arrival originates from a bunch of different festivals and celebrations from around the world. There may be certain objects, decorations, food, or music that we want to have present at our celebrations in order to warm our hearts with happy memories. We may recreate events, such as going caroling, having an open-house, watching a certain holiday movie, or joining in the annual reading of a poem or activity. Your traditions are not necessarily like anyone else's, and that's fine! Sharing our differences can make the holidays more interesting.

As generations grow forward, the ways our children celebrate holidays will inevitably change. Everyone in the family makes contributions to the construction of the holiday's meaning in their own way. It's important to involve children in the construction of the holiday. Their contributions may start out small, like decorating cookies or hanging ornaments on the tree. Over time, children figure out how to make bigger contributions to festive celebrations filled with memories they will carry forward. As children make their contributions, big or small, seeing people compliment them is important. This teaches them to be grateful and to compliment others for their graciousness to them. Over time, learning to share the attitude of gratitude with others will serve them well.

Just as we craft our holidays to be emotionally meaningful, it's good to remember that Santa and the elves are technically crafts-people. They work in their North Pole headquarters making toys. Helping children to craft objects to share with others as holiday gifts embody a very important process. Crafting presents for others is important for a variety of reasons. The process begins by helping children to think about what others would like. They may contemplate design or color factors. As they take their hands to craft the object, they are thinking about the person. Perhaps they dream about what they will say when they receive it, how they will look when they use it, and how happy they will be every time they look at it. Giving a hand-made gift is much more meaningful than going to the store and spending Mom and Dad's money to pick something out. Having parents buy a gift for someone that the child just puts their name on doesn't involve them in the emotional process of how to craft a meaningful gift and create a relationship with someone.

Ultimately, the Santa Spirit is of one caring. The Santa character empowers children to learn what it means to care about someone. This means figuring out what we can contribute to the well-being of others. Contributions can be time, effort, money, or doing good for others. Santa opens people's hearts to express loving-kindness that enables children to feel cherished, a very important Santa Spirit C-word. Now, isn't that a wonderful gift for children to receive?

6

$\mathcal{D}$

Dream, Delight, Donation, Dedication

The importance of dreaming is engrained into the whole Santa experience. Parents are encouraged to tuck wee ones in bed early on Christmas Eve so "visions of sugarplums" can "dance through their heads". Dreaming is akin to creating a movie in our minds about the way we want the future. It contains a whole sequence of images and events. When we dream about Santa, he seems alive and we can almost hear the sound of tiny reindeer hoofs on the rooftop. We can experience heart-thumping excitement, and almost feel the cold breeze on our faces and aren't sure if what we experienced really happened or not.

It's fun to dream, and Santa provides good inspiration. Children aren't the only ones who do it. Adults dream about how it will be when that special someone falls in love with us, how great that new job will be, or how lovely it would be to be rocked to sleep in a glorious sailboat during a seaside vacation. Dreams don't care if things are possible or plausible. While hope grounds people in likely scenarios, dreams may be totally groundless and quite impossible. It doesn't matter. Dreams aren't expected to be rational, logical, or based in reality. As Eleanor Roosevelt reportedly pointed out, "the future belongs to those who believe in the beauty of their dreams". Children benefit from learning that sometimes dreams come true. One dream-come-true can create a lifetime of joy and be enough to satisfy the soul to continue the act of reaching for the stars.

The potential of dreams coming true nurtures a sense of delight. When was the last time you felt delighted about something? Isn't it the most spectacular feeling? It is an utter joy, happiness without bounds, an enjoyment that is free and flowing. Santa helps children experience the kind of joy that adults have all-too-often forgotten. It's not that adults can't be delighted, but we have misplaced their ability to let go of the everyday burdens that possess us. Thankfully, children have not yet allowed bills and jobs, and other people's expectations control them. Children know how to live in the moment. They let go and are free. They know that life is a miracle and that the most amazing and remarkable things happen every day. Their joyous emotions flow like rivers through the family, sweeping everyone up in their adventures.

Helping children to share the joy with others, to donate it, to give it away freely, is another D Santa Spirit word. Donating, or giving something we value to others, is part of learning the Santa Spirit. Neighbors who didn't expect to be remembered are thrilled when there is a knock at the door and they find a plate of frosted cookies with ribbon wrapped around. Children with pets may find it delightful to donate to the humane society. Children may donate a favorite toy so other children can enjoy it. Some make potholders to give to people so they won't burn their fingers as they cook. The options for donating are endless. Donations need not be material and could be the donating of time to take care of a garden, to read a story, or to play a game with someone who needs cheer. Through giving is receiving, with the most delightful things never wrapped up in a box, but encased in our hearts.

Santa provides everyone in the family with the chance to experience delight Adults infused with the spirit of Santa share the recipes for how to make delight possible. When parents easily experience joy themselves, they make it possible for their children to be joyful too. Once we've experienced it, the potential for joy remains inside of us forever. Santa gives us an opportunity to remember that it's there.

7

E

Entertainment, Engagement, Excitement, Empathy

Believing in Santa Claus – or more exactly, the Santa Spirit – can engage us in thinking and doing actions that thoroughly entertain us. Many people enjoy decorating their homes, making gingerbread houses, or hosting holiday parties for family and friends. They are engaged in the process and spend lots of time and effort in creating events that will please and delight others. They get a sense of excitement in pulling off pleasing holiday events.

We may spend countless hours being entertained shopping online or in stores trying to find the perfect gift for someone. We are doing this because we care about them and want to make them happy. When we finally find "the one", we get excited and experience happy feelings inside. We may whisper secrets about what we are giving to someone, and exchange enthusiastic emotions about how excited they will be when we give it to them. In all honesty, we are likely putting forth all this effort as much for ourselves than for others because we enjoy it.

Working with children to engage the Santa Spirit can be totally engrossing and entertaining to both them and us. It's fun to concoct a plan together and implement it. At every stage of its development, we can have fun. But the best part about it is by engaging in exciting activities to make someone happy we are teaching children how to learn about empathy. Empathy is the ability to understand the feelings of another person and to use that understanding to guide our actions. When we sit with children (or ourselves) and contemplate what someone would truly like and how we could get it for them, we are employing empathy in action.

Most people appreciate receiving a thoughtful present that someone took the time to really think about much more than getting a gift card. Receiving something meaningless, given just to give "something", doesn't warm our heart. If we receive a re-gifted item that somebody didn't want and they gave it to us just to fulfill what they felt was an obligation to give us something, it doesn't feel very good. We don't feel we matter.

The real cost of a gift is in what it took from our time and thought, not necessarily what it took out of our wallet. Gifts that matter most come from genuine, loving concern. When someone spends time thinking about what we'd really enjoy or benefit from, it shows in their eyes, their smile, their eagerness to please us. At those moments, it doesn't matter to us if the gift is the wrong size or we already have one like it – knowing how hard someone tried to please us makes us cherish the gift because we feel cherished by someone we love.

Dr. Roman Krznaric, an international empathy advisor to

the United Nations and former professor at Cambridge University, notes that while the 20th century was the Age of Introspection where people focused on understanding themselves, the 21st century should become the Age of Empathy when we discover ourselves through becoming interested in the community and the lives of others. This shift in focus is part of a larger social transformation that contextualizes why the person of Santa Claus needs to be replaced with the spirit of Santa. This change shifts the focus from me as an individual to us as a social community. Thus, the focus on the Santa Spirit is actually part of a larger revolution in human relationships.

Empathy is essential in developing and maintaining healthy, happy relationships. Showing children how to develop empathy through the use of the Santa Spirit is a very good gift indeed. It is something that will serve them, and others, well for a long time to come.

8

F

Family, Friends, Fun, Food, Faith, Forgiveness

Throughout history, all around the world festivities that have morphed into the arrival of a Santa Claus figure have all been family and community-focused. The patterns they share include family and friends getting together, sharing specially prepared foods served only once a year, decorating their homes with lights, greenery, and color, giving each other little gifts, singing, dancing, having theatrical performances, laughing, and sharing good conversation. These gatherings are designed to foster fun and frolicking. Most families incorporate some traditions that they carry on year after year. These get-togethers are predictable annual occurrences to which everyone looks forward.

Youngsters may be given gifts. Adults may go out of their way to play games. Children come to love holidays as a result. As they get older, children assume more responsibilities carrying forth family traditions. Ultimately they transition from eating at the children's table to assuming their place with adults. The value of the interactions that occur at these family gatherings ought not to be diminished. Children are constant watchers of adult behavior and are primed to replicate what they see. Some actions are instrumental, like how to do things like get the tree to stand up straight in the stand, while some are expressive, like how one is to express gratitude. This is why it's important for adults to be on their best behavior at family gatherings! Adults teach them how to make special foods and learn the steps of traditional dances. Elders enjoy re-living their own childhoods as they watch the newest generations. Sharing stories, customs, and passing on the legacy of their families and cultures are woven into the tapestry of the celebrations. In this way, every member of the family plays an important role in the transmission of holiday celebrations from one generation to the next. Everyone gains something of relational importance from these annual gatherings.

As much as we love our families, bumps and conflicts arise during the year. There are some family members that we feel closer to or estranged from. Holiday gatherings provide an annual opportunity to get together and forgive the past. The essence of the Santa Spirit can help people to overcome tension and move forward anew with joy, loving-kindness, and forgiveness. When people carry the spirit of altruism and cheer in their hearts it can overpower defensiveness, hurt, and anger. This is of utmost importance. Children may know that tension between certain people exists; for them to watch healing occur sends a positive message of how to forgive.

Children and we as adults, all benefit by having faith that we will all get together again at the next arrival of Santa Claus.

Having faith that everyone will behave, that we will all have grown-up enough to let good cheer, wise words, helpful hands, and loving hearts predominate is something the Santa Spirit can inspire.

9

G

Goodness, Gladness, Gifts, Giving, Grace, Gratitude

Children giggle with gladness and gush with gratitude when their dreams come true on Christmas morning. Learning how to give and get gifts gracefully is an art that children will benefit from learning. Watching adults exhibit generosity and gratitude are great places to start. Children may learn to be greedy, another G-word, but could just as easily learn how to be gracious, a better G-word.

Some Santa Claus stories emphasize being "good for goodness sake". This is an interesting thing for the Santa Spirit to dissect. Teaching children that doing kind acts, even if no one sees, inspires self-control. Doing thoughtful things for others, just because they're nice, is fundamental in every religious tradition. Santa's arrival to deliver gifts when children are asleep reinforces the notion that he doesn't need or want to be seen when he's doing something good – he's delivering gifts just because he wants to make children happy. While he undoubtedly appreciates a good cookie, he doesn't expect gifts in return. He's exhibiting loving-kindness just because it's a noble thing to do.

It is important to let children know that striving to be good is important, but that nobody is good all the time. Everyone makes mistakes, even parents and teachers. Well-intended people mess up or sometimes act naughty. Threatening children that "Santa won't come" if they are less-than-perfect need to be reconsidered. It's when we make mistakes that we learn what we did wrong and how to learn to do better. A more constructive message is that everyone screws up sometimes, but the Santa Spirit focuses on how we try to be better, and help others to be better too.

The relationships between goodness, giving, and getting are seen in Secret Santa activities that many schools encourage. Children draw names of someone to do nice things for. They may not know or even like the other child, but by observing them, quietly getting to understand them, and gaining empathy for them, they are able to give them little things that may uplift their hearts. In this way, the Secret Santa activities actually benefit the giver more than the receiver. But we don't tell children that! This is another way for them to learn the importance of "show don't tell".

Learning how to be a generous giver and a grateful getter doesn't come naturally. Children have to observe adults doing this to see how it's done. They benefit from having opportunities to practice being a graceful giver and a graceful getter. Watching adults express the attitude of gratitude when they are given gifts is a very good way to spread the Santa Spirit. Observing adults who demand expensive things for themselves, or get upset when the gift they receive doesn't please them, role-model messages that are not in the Santa Spirit.

Parents often get stuck on the Santa-gifting thing, so let's clarify this. Santa drives a little sleigh that can't possibly hold many or big presents for every child. He has to travel all around the world giving to others. Thus logically the number, size, and amount of gifts "from Santa" should be quite limited. Stocking gifts are good Santa gifts. Let big or expensive presents come from the parents or grandparents who give them. Parents are the primary gift-givers and need to put their name on gifts, not Santa's.

There are a variety of different ways parents can gift children in meaningful ways. Be conscious of the symbolic message of how many and what we give to children. The type sends them expectations – thus books, art supplies, music, dolls, guns, and games all convey different messages. See the book, ***Re-Imagine Santa***, for more details about gifting!

Generosity to families who can't afford to gift their children is part of the Santa Spirit. So is down-sizing what we give to our own children in the name of Santa Claus. Showing children how to be gracious and have gratitude is within the realm of possibility. We have an opportunity to transform him into a spirit of gentle generosity, inclusion, and humanity. How cool is that?

10

H

Hospitality, Home, Harmony, Helpfulness, Hope

All the traditional celebrations that contributed to the creation of Santa incorporated hospitality. They were welcoming events, festivals where everyone could come together to share the common challenges of getting through cold, dark winters. Environmental conditions shaped people's experiences; they learned that helping each other was essential in order to survive. Annual winter celebrations allowed people to put work aside for a day, shelve interpersonal challenges, and focus on being happy. Neighbors helped each other to create events that brought people together in harmony. People opened their homes and welcomed others. Breaking bread, dancing, singing, exchanging gifts were heart-warming commonalities that have become part of holiday traditions.

Remnants of these community-wide winter solstice festivals continue throughout the world. People hurry "home for the holidays" because that's where they left happy memories that they hope to rediscover again. We go hoping that we will find harmony in these happy home-comings, that loved-ones still care about our humanity and will have real and true conversations loving conversations with us. We may look forward to helping cut down the tree, carve the turkey, or find out how to generate helpfulness to those we love when we don't see them often. The saying that "home is where the heart is" resonates loudly during holidays. We hope that we will find we still matter to them.

The Santa Spirit H words of honor, humanity, and hope emerge as important considerations. People everywhere long for the same things – to have a home to live in, enough food and safe water to consume, a way to make a meaningful contribution to their community, and to be loved and respected. Having respect for the diversity in every family, in every community, is part of honoring humanity. Finding ways to celebrate and honor the similarities and differences between and among us is essential in living in a humane world. The Santa Spirit embraces the hope that we can do that. Respect for humanity could be imparted to children everywhere. It will generate hopeful hospitality for the sake of this glorious planet that we all call home.

11

9

Imagination and Inspiration

Santa inspires curiosity, which enables children to use their imaginations to figure out things they didn't previously know. The notion of magical flying reindeer who can circle the world in a single night is filled with food for fantasy and discovery. How DO they do that? The Santa story is rich with opportunities to discover scientific information like how much a sleigh could hold, the speed of light, or mathematics about how many toys Santa would need to build for each child in the world to receive two. Children may wonder how Santa knows what size they wear and how he can make it around the whole world in a single night without sleeping or peeing. These questions naturally arouse interest. Santa is far from ordinary, and by being extraordinary he generates incredible inquisitiveness. Is his beard real? Which kind of cookie is his favorite? Does he have a favorite reindeer? Where do elves come from? How big is his toy shop? How does it feel to zoom into clouds in a sleigh? Children can tell you the answers to because the Santa story gives them rich opportunities to use their imaginations.

Imaginations enable us to become scientists of sorts as we explore possibilities and options. When children imagine how Santa could fit down a chimney, they develop hypotheses that they then assess – maybe one explanation doesn't seem feasible but another one does, especially if parts of it are tweaked. Maybe he has the ability to change shape or turn into a vapor that then rematerializes; maybe he has the talent to walk through walls; children can weigh out options and explore what could be real and why or why not. Thus Santa provides children with multiple opportunities to explore fantasy, reality, and possibility when they imagine.

It is important to remember that imagination is not a *thing*, but a process. Imagination scholars compare it to a muscle; without proper exercise and use, it will atrophy and cease to be functional. It must be nurtured in order to grow and develop. Robert Fulghum, author of *All I Ever Needed To Know I Learned In Kindergarten*, believes that imagination is stronger than knowledge and that myth is more potent than history. He believes that allowing children to build strong imaginations is a gift that parents can give them - and Santa is a gift to parents because he inspires that process to occur.

Deep down inside, children know that what they imagine may not be real. They are pretending. Pretending is fun. It's also good for children. Figuring out for themselves what is real from what isn't is an important step in children's growth. Children love to talk with one another about Santa and compare notes about what they believe he is like. Through their conversations children are provided the chance to think for themselves about what Santa is, what he isn't, and to weigh plausible explanations. Usually, there is no need for parents to delve into the "Santa isn't really real" conversation because children who can use their imaginations probably have already figured that out for themselves. Learning how to find answers to big questions on their own is important for their cognitive growth and development. This is why it is much better to give children space and time to figure out for themselves how Santa operates. They will benefit from it.

Nothing can ever be accomplished without imagination. Good imaginations are essential for doing well in school, on the job, and for being a success in life. You cannot create anything you want from life if you cannot see it as a possibility. In order for your dreams to manifest into reality, you must have a distinct vision to help you navigate through life.

Imaginations allow children to explore why things can have multiple meanings. They can learn that the occurrences in the Santa story can be explained from different points of view. They will contemplate whether Santa is a real person or really a spirit. Once they develop different interpretations for Santa, they will be able to take that skill and transform it into new uses, like coming up with different interpretations for people's behaviors or alternative explanations for how things work. A curiosity of Santa can lay the foundation for scientific thought, as well as an appreciation for things that exist that can't quite be proved – like love.

12

J

Joy

Joy is the quintessential Santa Spirit word. In many people's minds, joy and happiness are words for the same thing – but they aren't. While Santa Claus might deliver happiness, the Santa Spirit can bring us joy.

We are happy when Santa or our friend gives us the book we wanted or a toy that is fun to play with. We are happy when we get candy to eat or when relatives visit us. Happiness is an emotion, one generated from external circumstances, events, or other people's behaviors. Happiness is thus momentary and short-lived. When we write our letters to Santa, we may ask for certain things, like a pony, with the caveat that "if I had it, then I would be truly happy". Adults do this kind of pleading all the time – we think that if we land a certain job, get married, or purchase the car we always wanted, then we will be happy. Advertisers tell us that if we buy certain sneakers, use certain drugs, eat certain products or use a fitness app that we will get healthier, which will make us more attractive to others and bring happiness.

The problem with happiness is that it's externally driven and short-lived. Once the candy is eaten, the toy breaks, the shoes wear out, or the perfect person we dreamed of having in our lives isn't so perfect after all, happiness can evaporate. Happiness is quite fickle. Any time we look for an external occurrence to make us happy, we should realize that happiness is time-limited. We may go looking for other toys, foods, cars, jobs, or relationships to make us happy as a result, but suspect that they too may disappear in the long run.

Joy is an emotion too but stems from an internal state that we have control over. Joy isn't dependent upon someone else's behavior or outside events. It cannot be bought. It's not externally based like happiness. It is an internal way of seeing and living in the world that is constant and not contingent upon anyone or anything else. It stems from gratitude and the appreciation of the big meaning found in little things. When we are content and at peace, regardless of what others think or what others are doing, we set the conditions to find joy.

Unlike happiness that can disappear in a flash, joy can be long-lasting. Joy can exist even when happiness doesn't exist since our emotional state isn't dependent upon outside situations or people. Even when things turn in directions we didn't want them to and we may not be happy, we can still experience joy. It is the idea that in dark times happiness flees, but even during difficult times when we feel upset or sad, joy can still remain. This is because joy is related to the beauty of human connection, good intentions, and understanding and acceptance of ourselves and others. When we live with a joyful heart it is easier to show love and respect to others and ourselves. There are no promises that life will always be easy. But it is possible to find the joy that peaceful acceptance can bring. This is why joy is always better than happiness to cultivate.

Children grow and new ones arrive. Santa may feel happiness bringing a certain child a certain gift, but both of them move along in life and are ever-changing. Yet Santa's joy doesn't diminish when the holiday is over. The Santa Spirit maintains internal peace and pleasantness and is constant from one month to another, year after year. The Santa Spirit keeps working forward when we get tired because there is some greater good we experience rather than some momentary pleasure.

The Santa Spirit will help us find joy rather than happiness, which most people find to be a lot better in the long run. When we act in the Santa Spirit this may require that we engage ourselves to use hope, to be patient, to be gentle with ourselves and others, and to control ourselves to continue to show children the Santa Spirit, not just talk about what to do. If children – and adults – can learn to seek joy instead of happiness, every day could feel like the magic we hope to find at Christmas.

13

K

Kindness

The Santa Spirit is merely a key (Santa Spirit K-word) to unlock the loving-kindness (the main Santa Spirit K word) potential that resides in all of us. Inside of every living being is a soul that longs to be happy and loved. Just as we feel better when our hearts are open, we can assume that others want to express loving-kindness and they too feel better when they receive it.

Showing children how to have a tender heart is part of wise parenting. Of course, it is best if we express the Santa Spirit all year long, not just in December. But as the December holidays approach, they provide an annual opportunity to go out of our way to do better in showing people that we care. Parents and adults engage children to find ways to help soften the burdens carried by those who are poor, sick, and suffering. Expressing generosity towards the animals counts too. Taking care of the earth and doing our share to be wise stewards of the planet matters. We hold the keys to unlock countless doors that could open up the Santa Spirit. Parents and adults are in positions of power to show (not just tell) children how to create and implement the spirit of loving-kindness that is inherent in the Santa Spirit.

Children are watching everything we say and do. They see when we're cranky, they watch us when we smile, children know when adults have been bad or good – so be good for goodness sake, Mom and Dad! When we use our words carefully to say respectful things to or about others, children hear. When adults use harsh tones and cutting statements we are teaching children this is an acceptable, and expectable, way to talk to people we don't like. The very words we speak convey whether the Santa Spirit will be present in our homes and in children's heads.

The fact that we hold the keys to unlock the Santa Spirit is something we ought to remember. Like the butterfly effect, we have the keys to unleashing the Santa Spirit to spread around the world by what we say and what we do.

Before children disremember they have magic inside, their giggles and sweetness can melt the ice around the heart of the crankiest person. Children have an intimate relationship knowing the Santa Spirit. It is us adults who have forgotten it. This is why it's important for adults to rediscover the Santa Spirit inside of us. When others unlock the Santa Spirit in their heart, it helps us to unlock it in ours. When we all evoke the Santa Spirit, it helps people of every age to overcome obstacles and open up to kinder conversations and make life a lot more fun.

14

L

Light, Listen, Learn, Legacy, Love

Let's start with the word light since all of the winter solstice festivals focus on bringing light into the home. Winter solstice is the shortest daylight – longest darkness day of the year. Bringing light into darkness lifts the spirit and brings us hope for brighter tomorrows. Lights can be found with the use of candles, lights on trees or strung around the home, lights placed in windows, outside community bonfires, Kwanza, Advent or Menorah-lit candles or visits from Santa coming down the chimney. Shining light into our homes and our hearts is part of the Santa Spirit. They are beautiful and help us to remember that we too have a beautiful light inside just waiting to be lit ablaze.

The Santa Spirit encourages us to listen to each other, especially at holiday time, to hear what we need and want. We can't automatically know what would please others. Often we talk in "code" with one another. When a child or person of any age brings up a topic to talk about, they are doing so because that topic matters to them in some important way. We may put out a hint to see if anyone picks up on it. This is why we have to listen to each other not just with our ears but with our hearts. It takes time to engage in real listening. It has to be done wholeheartedly. We have to ask questions to find out why the person brought the topic up in the first place. For instance, when a child asks for something, it may be for their own enjoyment, but it could also be for something that is for someone else, or a gift that would enable them to do something for others. If people talk about a particular person or incident, it is because they matter. We don't talk about things that don't matter to us. Sometimes tender topics are introduced gently to see if others will respond in a kindly, thoughtful way. Thus spending time to really sit down and listen to children, or our partner, our co-workers, or neighbors, really matters.

When we do, we could learn (another L word) a great deal. There's always a lot to learn when we use the Santa Spirit. Sometimes the learning comes from books, sometimes from movies or toys, we may receive. Then there is the learning about each other. Time together during the holidays often gives us opportunities to talk together and find out new things about each other. The old saying that "still waters run deep" can be quite true when it comes to really talk to family and people we think we know. Maybe we will learn that we don't know as much about each other as we thought we did. There is only one way to find out – and that is to talk and listen.

Ultimately, the holidays set forth the building of family legacies and traditions that can get carried forward for years, perhaps even hundreds of years through countless generations.

If we consider that the holidays are a prime time to build memories, then use the Santa Spirit to make them positive ones. Most people remember holidays or events that were sour, sad, heart-breaking. Make no sad if you can. The Santa Spirit's focus on love – the ultimate L word – is the gift that most of us want most of all. The best way to get love is to give it. And that L word is free for everyone to give.

15

M

Merriment, Miracles, Marvel, Meaning

Merry Christmases, Hanukkahs, Kwanzas, and other festivities don't just happen organically. They are made (a M-word). To make merry is a universal process that people engage in when they want to celebrate or make an event special. Families can develop their own merry-making style. A designated time can be selected that everyone knows is the moment for the merrymaking, while it happens spontaneously in other families. Making-merry can be a verb when no work, no drama, no tension, or woes are allowed. Usually, merry-making includes special foods, drinks, decorations, and activities. The notion that for however long you decide to make merry, the goal is for everyone to have fun and be pleasant sharing the Santa Spirit with each other.

Another key in good merry-making is for everyone to participate in the decision of what it means to be having fun. Successful merry-making is a participatory, democratic activity in which everyone can engage. If one parent or person decides unilaterally the details of what is going to happen in the merriment, it raises the chances that other members may be alienated. No matter how young or old the members need to have input to help craft the event and the opportunity to actively participate in it. Diversity in the activities will help create the possibility that there is something for everyone, and that no one person takes charge when it becomes "all about them". What this means that it is important to create a merriment opportunity that everyone can find meaningful.

When everyone feels engaged and cared about, it increases the chances they will act in the Santa Spirit. The warmth of the Santa Spirit increases the chances that family members will marvel at how much better people are getting alone. What makes for a "marvelous" holiday may be perceived differently by everyone.

When families who have been estranged or who have hardened their hearts become more open when exposed to the Santa Spirit, it brings both happiness and joy that can be so great it feels to be a miracle. A miracle, by definition, is an unlikely event that occurs which brings very welcome consequences to everyone. Miracles seem more likely to happen when people use the Santa Spirit. We may be surprised, amazed at how something so little yet so extraordinarily big changes our expectations in a very happy way. Sometimes people feel miracles are caused by divine intervention. But we can create miracles for people too. We can create peace where there was war. We can create abundance when there was poverty. The meanest, hardhearted person can become kind, as Ebenezer Scrooge and the Grinch showed us. Softening our hearts, thus, can perhaps be the biggest miracle of all. The Santa Spirit gives us a tool to help that happen.

16

N

Nature and Neighbors

The winter festivals occurring around the world that gave rise to the Santa figure worked in tandem with nature and the environment. The natural world was people's guide for what to expect in the days to come and how to prepare for them. Neighbors banded together to get through tough times and to celebrate the good ones.

Think about the many different nature symbols used in winter solstice festivals! As a game with the family, people could consider their own cultures and traditions and see how nature influenced the creation of the celebrations. These included the revolutions of the earth around the sun, the placement of the moon, and the prediction of when there would be warmth and sun or darkness and cold. People used the stars to know when to plant and when to harvest. Stars, moon, and twinkling lights in the sky were routinely used by sailors and seers to predict the future. People routinely watched the migration patterns of the birds to see when cold weather was coming and when spring was on its way. The woolly caterpillar has been used by the Old Farmer's Almanac for decades to predict what kind of weather we are going to have.

Greenery, with ferns, firs, holly, ivy, pine, spruce, or vines are used worldwide to form trees, wreaths, or garlands. Icicles and berries have been used to adorn the greenery. Reindeer, horses, goats, donkeys, buffalo, hedgehogs, pigs, and cats have all become part of winter holiday traditions. In December there are many different days designated to honor animals, such as the World Wildlife Conservation Day (Dec. 4), National Day of Animal Rights (Dec. 10), National Day of the Horse (Dec. 13), Monkey Day (Dec. 14) or Visit the Zoo Day (Dec. 27). Ravens are central to winter solstice stories, as are doves, the bluebird of happiness, red-breasted robins, and roosters. Acorns have been gifted as symbols of good luck. Sand dollars contain little doves of peace that can be released when they are broken. There are other nature symbols that people may not automatically think about. For instance, spider webs were the foundation for tinsel. Pine cones became ornaments, as have painted eggshells. Pomegranates, apples, carrots, chili peppers, peanuts and pickles, and oranges are winter solstice specific foods, and the yule log, roses, and poinsettias adorn our houses. And of course, we cannot forget the importance of mistletoe!

Living in harmony with nature is part of the Santa Spirit. Listening to the wind, reading the skies, understanding the flights of the birds or the turning of the leaves reminds us that we are all one, confronting the same elements and challenges every day. When we work with nature, and one another, things go more smoothly. As neighbors, we realize we are all one family under one roof, one sky, drinking from the same streams and eating the same corn. We depend upon one another. Santa's story working with his reindeer and flying through the cold, dark sky shows how miracles can occur when we live in harmony with the natural elements. Taking good care of the planet and all its beings, big and small, is part of the Santa Spirit.

17

O

Opportunity, Open-minds & hearts, Oneness

If we open our minds to the options for creating goodness, we discover that our choices are limitless. In whatever ways we decide to use our gifts and talents, if we are open-hearted and open-minded, we can use the season leading up to Santa's arrival to be overwhelmingly wonderful for those we care about.

The Santa Spirit is a vehicle that gives us an opportunity for us to show people we care. It provides an opportunity to share and create positive bonds. Practicing the Santa Spirit in front of children demonstrates what it means to live joyfully, kindly, and altruistically. Showing the Santa Spirit to our neighbors, colleagues, and others set a standard of how we believe people ought to treat one another. This is sweetly demonstrated in Patricia Polaco's book, *Trees of the Dancing Goats*, where people in a small town help one another to celebrate their holidays, even though the holidays are different from their own. When we seize the opportunity to act in open-hearted kindness to others, it can raise the bar for others to reach deep into themselves to show their own goodness. Simple exchanges like this have tremendous power in being able to improve community climate and help us to reach across differences to find the common goodness that we share.

One of the most common images of Santa is of him having a sleigh full of treasures and pulling goodies out of his sack. This notion of abundance has stuck in our minds for a reason. It symbolically conveys that there is more goodness in people's hearts that could possibly be contained, so much goodness that it overflows and spills out onto the floor and into the world. This sense of having more than enough at least once a year can give a child optimism that tomorrow could also be full of the good things of life.

The best O Santa Spirit word to remember is Oneness. Indeed, we are all unique, different in our appearance, backgrounds, and experience. Those differences are to be respected and appreciated. Yet the Santa Spirit helps us to remember that between us we have more that is the same. We all need food, water, and shelter. We want to be free from sickness and suffering. We all want to be loved. We don't want anyone to hurt us or those we love. We want to experience both peace and joy. What the Santa Spirit does is help us to figure out how to enhance those universal needs so that we can all be lifted up. If we were all lifted up – imagine how much happier and healthier our families and communities could be. This is a wondrous opportunity that could be within our reach.

18

$\mathcal{P}$

Process, Parenting, Planning, Play, Patience

By now in the alphabet search, it should be clear that the Santa Spirit isn't connected with a person, culture, religion, or ideology. Focusing on the 24 days building up to the arrival of Santa Claus is helpful because it gives us time to consider how we will create a joyful holiday season. If we want it to be meaningful for ourselves and others, then we have the power to construct it to achieve that outcome.

The Santa Spirit is a process of how we interact with others. It gives us the opportunity to process what we want ourselves and the world to be like. By processing our true wants and desires, we realize that what we want can't fit into Santa's sleigh or sack. It can't be bought or sold. The spirit of Santa can only emerge when we fill our hearts with tenderness and lovingkindness. It arises when our minds are open to listening, looking, and understanding the world from other people's perspectives. The December holidays, however you celebrate them, provides us with an opportunity to step back, take a breath, and contemplate how we want to use the time to improve the lives of others. The ironic thing is that as we focus on helping others, we end up helping ourselves.

If Process is the key P Santa Spirit word, there are partner words of parenting, planning, play, and patience. As adults, whether we have biological children or not, we are in the position of parenting others. The Latin root word of parenting is parere, which means to give birth to or to produce. Every one of us is responsible for producing care for the wellbeing of children. It means helping children to be the best they can be as they grow. Since we all remember our childhood in our hearts and minds, we can use the Santa Spirit to reflect upon all the people who parented us well along our journey to adulthood. We are all in positions of having the opportunity to influence how children see themselves, others, and the world. We are their providers and protectors, either directly or indirectly, through the policies and practices we advocate for or deny them access to. We are their teachers, maybe officially or often informally, as we role-model how to act and what they should think.

Good parenting isn't haphazard. It takes planning, thought, and commitment. It includes a hearty dose of patience. It needs to incorporate play, which is essential for them and for us. So much of life is predicated upon production, and even young children aren't immune from pressures to practice today for what they will become tomorrow. Playing enables us to enjoy the moment and each other.

If we are totally honest with ourselves, all we have is this moment. Any of us can be gone in a flash. Accidents, viruses, health conditions all can snap away our lives. We can never get today back. Wise parents know this, which inspires us to process how we can use the opportunities surrounding Santa's arrival to produce positivity that may lodge in children's heads and hearts forever.

19

Q

Quiet

The Q Santa Spirit word stands for the benefit of being quiet. We are often surrounded by so many sounds that we have forgotten the power of being quiet. It is when we are quiet that we can easily find the Santa Spirit. Quiet to listen to the tick of the clock, the purr of the cat, and the beating of our own heart. Quiet to contemplate the thoughts that rise up in our head and the emotions that swell up in our hearts when we are not chasing from here to there and back, only to find we are stuck in the same place over and over. Quiet to hear what our powerful inner voice is screaming in whispers for us to pay attention to.

It's hard to listen to the internal quiet when we are constantly inundated with the external noise. Telephones, televisions, radios, social media, and computers fill almost every minute of every day with chatter. In our homes, schools, stores, and workplaces, it seems as though someone is always talking. As we travel down the street, there is the constant hum of traffic, orders from the GPS, lyrics from songs, or announcements from advertisers. There is so much constant noise that we have become immune to it. We don't even hear it anymore. And when there is quiet, we may not know what to do with it, and even feel quite uncomfortable with it. It is as though we have to fill the void with more noise as we have not become friends with the quiet.

But quietness can become one of our best friends. If someone is always making noise, then how can we hear ourselves think? What inside us has been relegated to whispers, all-but-drowned-out by the constant barrage of external noise? Quiet is sometimes most easily found by sitting and doing nothing. We need to remember that doing nothing is actually doing something and that doing nothing could be doing something quite important indeed. Quiet means learning to be patient since what is trying to escape into our brains has been pushed down so deep for so long that it's going to take it some time to find its way home.

So often we learn as children that we must be productive, that doing nothing is a sign of laziness that must be avoided. But the Santa Spirit knows that quiet is essential. If you can't find it inside, you can't use it. If you don't share the Santa Spirit, we all suffer. Thus we need to imagine Santa sitting in a big, comfortable chair in front of an ember-glowing fireplace sipping a mug of steamy hot chocolate. Santa knows that working hard has its place – but so does being quiet. It is then when we can rejuvenate not just our bodies but our hearts and minds.

Encourage children to experience and appreciate quiet. The best way to show them is to do it ourselves. Making friends with quiet is part of the Santa Spirit.

20

R

Reality, Re-define, Revitalize, Respect

An age-old question confronting parents is – Is Santa Real? This is what the Santa Spirit seeks to address. An actual blood-and-bones, breathing, walking, talking person named Santa Claus who lives in the North Pole with elves and reindeer isn't real the same way that Grandpa who lives with his dog around the corner in a house that we visit. But Grandpa, Mom, our neighbor, or other people can be kind, altruistic, and do amazing things that surprise and delight us. They can be Santas by sharing the Santa Spirit. Thus, the spirit of Santa is real. That spirit has existed for hundreds of years and can be found all around the globe. The people who deliver it may not look the same, but the idea that there is a prototype of what a Santa is and does can be extrapolated and generalized to countless others. Any of us can act in the Santa Spirit. We are real, our fun, loving spirit is real, so in that sense, Santa is real too.

Santa Claus has always been a product of the ongoing social

construction of reality. His appearance has changed across time and place. He has been tall, short, chubby, skinny, male, female, with every skin color, found in every continent, wearing colors ranging from red to green to pink to brown. He has been either loved or maligned by clergy, political leaders, advertisers, and parents. He is what we choose to make him.

What we believe to be real will become real in its consequences. If we believe that Santa is real, he is. If we believe he isn't real, he's not to us. If we believe that Santa is kind, joyful, and thoughtful, we can make him into that. If we believe that Santa is a creepy drunk who inspires greed, exploits, or excludes certain children, that is indeed what we may see and create as a result. As adults and parents, we hold a tremendous amount of power over how we want children to see Santa.

As you contemplate how you will use the Santa Spirit to influence children's lives, we could give him a face-lift, a makeover, refresh his image and redefine him to be more inclusive, diverse, and demonstrate respect for every child of every type. Children of every ability, every race, nationality, gender, faith, appearance need to know that they are beloved, special and that adults care about them. Even if it is just for one moment of the year, experiencing an abundance of love can give us hope to sustain us through even the darkest times for the rest of our lives.

21

S

Santa Spirit & Santa Stocking

Today many families feel as though they don't have the money to have Santa come. Countless people are unemployed, losing their homes, have their incomes, and benefits cut due to health and economic woes. When Santa is associated with bringing lots of presents, many parents wonder if they can afford him to be part of their celebrations. It's easier to say he's not real and to shut-down the possibility that he exists. This is understandable.

A good way to explain Santa to children is to point out that it is impossible for him to bring all the children of the world big or many gifts since he travels in a sleigh pulled by tiny reindeer. Going back to his traditional image, in his sack he can pull out a few small things to put into children's stockings or shoes, but there is no way that he can give every child many or big items. He wants to give gifts to large numbers of children, which means that children need to be respectful of the fact that nobody gets many, big or expensive gifts from Santa. He ostensibly makes simple toys with the help of elves. They aren't a tech firm that makes computers, phones, tablets, or televisions. They're not reasonable to expect Santa to bring. If children get those kinds of things, it's because Mom and Dad went to the store and bought them. Most of the gifts that children may receive should logically come from family and friends – not Santa.

It is possible to include Santa as a happy holiday figure IF he is re-conceptualized as a spirit rather than a person. It is possible to give children a positive and meaningful gift of the Santa Spirit. This shift actually puts Santa back into his original form. Santa Claus was originally designed to bring forth the spirit of joy, altruism, family and community bonding, and hope for a brighter tomorrow. As shown throughout this book, the Santa Spirit encases a wide variety of positive attributes and actions that would increase the wellbeing of children. The Santa Spirit also gives adults a designated opportunity to rediscover and implement their own joy that comes from giving of themselves to others.

In the story, *The Legend of the Santa Stocking,* a multi-generational, economically struggling family is faced with the issue of how to gift one another for Christmas. The could-be-homeless aunt who has the least financial resource is the one who gives the family the greatest gift. She has the family sit together and write down things they really enjoy about one another on pieces of paper. It could be things like "I love the way you make me laugh", "You make the best cookies in the world", or "I like playing games with you – can we play one together soon?" Small children can draw pictures if they haven't yet the ability to write words. Everyone can tuck the many pieces of paper into each person's stocking to be opened on Christmas Day.

Having the opportunity to contemplate all the ways we appreciate one another is a good way to teach children to be thoughtful about all the wonderful ways people who love and care for them. Creating a stocking out of old socks, material, or even paper is easy and costs nothing. Decorate them the ways you like. Then on Christmas Eve, have everyone put into one another's stockings the slips of paper that say what we cherish about one another. Tucking them into the toe of the stocking, where Santa could put a few small objects on the top, makes three things possible. One, it ensures that everyone will receive a meaningful gift. Two, it will automatically limit the number and types of things that Santa can bring. Three, having the notes at the toe lets us "save the best for last" – which is learning about how dearly people love us.

The Santa Stocking has the potential of totally transforming what Santa Claus brings. If we all do it, it has the potential to foster equality for all, take materialism away from the message Santa can deliver, and focus on what people want most for Christmas - love. Love is free and easy to give and has the power to change the world.

22

T

Trust, Traditions, Tenderness, Thankfulness

Some parents say they don't want their children to believe that Santa is real because if they do, they will be lying to them. How can children trust us if we lie to them about Santa, they ask? Trust between parents and children is vitally important. This is where teaching children that anyone can share the Santa Spirit is important. In focusing on his fun, altruistic characteristics, children can learn that when they act in their highest goodness that anyone can become a Santa. For those of us who believe in the Santa Spirit, Santa is indeed real, and what he can deliver is really important. Learning that anyone and everyone has the capacity for loving-kindness is a valuable thing.

Children have the ability to appreciate fantasy and reality at the same time. For instance, millions are encouraged to see Mickey Mouse on television or meet him in person at Disneyland. Children know that Mickey isn't a real mouse, but he is real nonetheless. Santa is but one of the many figures that children who enjoy who is both real and not real at the same time; Big Bird isn't really a bird and Spider-Man can't really climb up skyscrapers but children enjoy playing with the idea that they could be real. "Let's go see Santa" isn't much different from "Let's go see Mickey". Santa gives children the opportunity to learn that things can be real in one way but not in another simultaneously. It's cognitively useful for children to stretch their imaginations to find joy. Truth all depends upon how we adults choose to define and portray what is real about Santa. Thus, it doesn't have to be a lie to believe in Santa – children could equally learn that he – or the spirit he delivers - is quite real and wonderful.

We must remember that Santa Claus is a transitional figure. He means different things to us at different times of our lives. Babies don't care about Santa – they are more intrigued by boxes and lights. Toddlers comprehend tangible things such as snow people, reindeer, and elves; Santa Claus may be perceived as a real person because children cannot yet grasp abstract concepts. He provides children with an opportunity to explore what is concrete and what is abstract and sets the stage for their cognitive development to later grapple with things like God. Older children use learning about mythical characters and engaging in make-believe to help them grapple with what is fantasy and what is real. Imagination is found to be critically important for creativity and later success. As children age, they learn more about history, science, and cause-and-effect relationships. They naturally will come to question the reality of Santa during this time, so adults don't have to worry about telling them "the truth", as there are many different iterations of it. Pondering the nature of reality is a logical process as we mature.

During young adulthood, Santa is less of an interest than building identity and friendships.

When people become parents, Santa re-emerges as an issue. Parents contemplate what parts of their own childhood they should pass on to their own children, and what parts should be re-invented or eliminated. Couples negotiate what Santa should mean to their children, and many choose to have fun incorporating him into their children's experiences. Middle-aged parents developmentally have a different view of Santa. If they are working several jobs and money is scarce, they may try to downplay Santa and gifts to children who are still small. The pressure on parents may just be too much for them to create magical, extensive holiday festivities. If there are no longer little ones at home to entertain by tantalizing them with the expectation of Santa's arrival, the holidays may become boring. Parents may find that they have to work harder to make the holiday meaningful. There may be less emphasis on putting gifts out on Christmas Eve when the children are in bed, fewer presents (or more gift cards) in the stockings of adult children, and less excitement on getting up early on Christmas morning to see if Santa arrived. They may seek alternative celebrations to replace the excitement that Santa once held. When people become grandparents, their orientations toward Santa shifts yet again. Babies bring new enthusiasm to adults, who again get to relive their childhoods and their children's childhoods as they prepare to celebrate for the arrival of Santa. Grandparents carry forth the potential of the legacy for carrying on Christmas traditions.

As people make their transitions from one age to another, the Santa figure takes on different meanings. He too makes transitions of what he is and what he means to us. The benefit of knowing about the Santa Spirit is that we can use the Santa character to teach different things to us across the lifespan. Santa can be just as meaningful for people who are older as he is to people who are young. Capturing the ability to be young at heart is a wonderful thing. Appreciating that what Santa means varies and takes on various dimensions can be helpful in bringing us joy.

23

U

Unique, Unselfish, Understanding

The obvious fact is that we are all unique. We do not look, act, or believe the same things. Our experiences and expectations are different. Even within our family, while we naturally have many similarities, we are all different. Some of us may be so uniquely different that we feel we don't even fit in. There are constant internal and external struggles imposed upon us about whether we should be like everyone else or go it alone in our uniqueness.

Human nature teases us to believe that our uniqueness is best. If it is best, then we want others to be like us. But in doing that, we strive to make everyone the same, which defeats the appreciation of our diversity. Understanding and appreciating the value of difference can be reflected in something as obvious as our eating styles. We want a salad – some of us are content with a quarter-head of iceberg lettuce, while most of us prefer a salad consisting of diverse ingredients. Maybe we want tomatoes, arugula, romaine, cucumbers, different types of peppers, carrots, radishes, onions, croutons, artichoke hearts, cheeses, nuts, eggs, fish, beans, corn or meats; few of us like everything, but most of us appreciate the salad when it's got some diverse elements in it.

Honoring the diversity between and among us is part of the natural order. Trees of different types grow strong side by side. Dogs of every species romp together harmoniously. Within our own body, scientists say we replace every cell in our body in seven to ten years – so even we aren't the same as we were from one moment to another. Even in our differences, while we may have more in common with some people than others, over 99% of our DNA is the same.

The Santa Spirit doesn't have to look the same for everyone. Every person acting in the Santa Spirit will have some things they like to contribute, things that they do well or want to try, while others have different preferences and contributions. That's fine! Just as every child and every adult are different, every person acting in the Santa Spirit is different. Nobody can be all things to all people. Finding our gifts and talents we want to share is important.

Some children are exposed to a vision of Santa Claus of someone who gives them oodles of expensive gifts. Others know Santa doesn't bring presents at all. Moving away from a Santa as the material gifter may help us to teach children to be unselfish and more keenly aware of the wide range of experiences of others. Children don't automatically come wired to be selfish or unselfish – these are characteristics they learn from observing others. Ultimately, separating Santa the person from Santa the spirit is essential in shifting the Santa Claus tradition away from material gifts to giving gifts of the heart. Understanding that we are unique will help us to be unselfish, thereby helping to capture the Santa Spirit and hold it, and each other, dear.

24

$\mathcal{V}$

Values

Values, our Santa Spirit V-word, are things the guide how we live, what we say, and what we do. What we value becomes extensions of ourselves. What the Dali Lama or Mother Teresa value becomes identified with who they are as human beings. Our values define us. What we value guides our actions.

The problem with values is what we say and do are often at great variance with each other. We can say we value peace, but are quick to get in a fight. We say we value fitness but don't exercise and choose unhealthy foods because we like them more. We can say we value freedom of speech but then tell people to shut up or go away when we don't like what they have to say. We may report that we think that children are the most important thing in the world to invest in because they are our future, yet we vote down funding a new school, cut free lunch and food stamp programs, don't support affordable, accessible high-quality daycare or preschools, and so on.

Every moment of every day we are choosing how to spend our energy, our time, and our money. Every thought we have sends a message about what we prioritize as important. Every word we utter tells others what we think and value. When someone is spewing forth anger and venom, it is apparent that loving-kindness towards others is not their top-level priority, no matter what they say.

The Santa Spirit emphasis during December helps remind us to put our actions where our mouth is. It encourages us to have the courage and motivation to put into action what we say we believe. It inspires us to be more generous with our time or money. As we visualize (another great V-word) what we want others to think of us, and what we want people to remember about us when we are gone, we can use the Santa Spirit as the opportunity to carry forth the suggestion by Mahatma Gandhi:

"We but mirror the world. All the tendencies present in the outer world are to be found in the world of our body. If we could change ourselves, the tendencies in the world would also change. As a man changes his own nature, so does the attitude of the world change towards him. This is the divine mystery supreme. A wonderful thing it is and the source of our happiness. We need not wait to see what others do."

25

W

Wonder, Waiting, Wisdom

Part of the beauty and magic of childhood is the ability to gaze upon the world with wonder. How did it come to pass that things are the way they are? How could things be different, and what would it require for those changes to occur? The innocence of childhood empowers us to see past what is and to consider what could be. That ability is wonderful in and of itself. Adults often lose it as they age. This is why children are essential in showing adults how to get the Santa Spirit.

Children are filled with awe, belief, curiosity, and the Santa Spirit from A to Z. Because adults have forgotten how to find it, they need reminders. One reminder is hanging around little children during the holiday. Children's ability to see what is real, and what is really important, is contagious. Adults find themselves on the floor, giggling, playing, and discovering what they have long disremembered.

This book is written to help adults to rediscover the wonderful wisdom that children embrace as normal, natural and the way things are. As we have gone from A to Z, the pages are filled with reminders of what we have too often buried inside of us. Like reindeer who paw their hoofs on the ground, eagerly waiting to take off and fly into the sky, the advent of Santa's arrival sets us free to go be ourselves again, at least for a little while. We take the time to focus on others. We contemplate generous or frivolous ways to make others happy. As we turn outward to give loving-kindness, we find we too become lighter, happier, and freer. Going through the holiday with the Santa Spirit in one's heart is a change-maker away from the holidays being seen as a burden and time of drudgery.

Knowing that they can look forward to Santa's annual visit, children learn the value and importance of waiting. There is great value in waiting. It allows for contemplation, planning, and the nurturing of wonder. They may keep part of the Santa Spirit active all year long.

But sometimes we adults don't. As waiting pertains to adulthood, it is easy to lose our childhood wonder. Our lives may have become like rats on a treadmill, working hard and going nowhere as we wonder how long we can go on like that. We wonder where the pot of gold at the rainbow's end can be found. This is why the 24 days before Santa's arrival is critically important for adults. It is a concrete reminder that we have an opportunity to get busy shifting our focus and actions to do for others – to be who we say we want to become.

The annual reminder of Santa's arrival circumvents the world and cuts across all faiths, ideologies, and political agendas. Children don't struggle with issues of difference or oneness because in their minds they are part and parcel of the same thing, like the yin and the yang. Wisdom in children is often automatic, pure, and true. As we grow forward, we acquire other and different types of wisdom. The arrival of Santa gives us an opportunity to rediscover the sweetness of childhood belief, joy, and wisdom once again.

26

X

XOXOXOXOXOXOXOXO

X stands for Hugs
Hug those you love
And hug the world with
The Santa Spirit

27

Y

You

The most important Y word is YOU. You have tremendous power to change the world. You have the daily choice to bring forth joy or suffering to yourself and others. You have the option of whether you will greet every person you meet with the Santa Spirit or whether you will be a grump or even heartless. You can choose the path of loving-kindness or not. You can decide if you will start spreading the Santa Spirit today, if you want to wait until tomorrow, or if it is a foolish thing to pursue at all. You are holding the future of the world right in your hand to do with as you please.

Children of every age are counting on YOU to show that you believe in the spirit of Santa in the very inclusive, flexible, respectful ways outlined in this book. Know that the thing that made people believe in Santa in the first place had nothing to do with an actual human being. The reason that people have believed in him so long is that they believe in the power of love and kindness that is inside of themselves – and you. If you can find the spirit in yourself, then you can give it to others so they can let their own goodness free to fly across the world. Imagine the ripple-out effects across the sky that the Santa Spirit could deliver.

28

Z

Zest and Zeal

Zest refers to having great enthusiasm for living life to the fullest, enjoying every moment of every day. When we have a zest for something we pour our whole heart and soul into what we are undertaking. It is an attitude that fosters action. We are not going through the motions; we are not spectators of life. Rather, we are thoroughly engaged in what we are doing. We fly through our days; we seem nimble as we scamper over obstacles that others would see as insurmountable challenges.

A companion word, zeal, refers to one's diligent devotion to eagerly and ardently pursuing something deemed of utmost importance. When we experience zeal, we may feel such a commitment that our pursuit gives us boundless energy. We become tireless, with a fervent commitment to do all we can to make something happen. Someone who is zealous may be entirely concerned with protecting something that to them is solid, true, good, and eternal. Zeal motivates the creation of zest. Without the drive or zeal, zest would not occur.

Santa has a zeal for making children all over the world happy. He works all year to make special that single night when he is able to bring magic to people's hearts. He isn't doing this because he has to; he has the burning desire to do whatever it takes to bring children joy. He doesn't carry out his zeal-motivated task as a burden but as extreme pleasure. He takes absolute delight in making merry. His life is filled with spirited enjoyment of what he is doing, rich with flavor and gusto. He must make merry; his zest for living is contagious and helps others to live more zestfully as well.

The Santa Spirit for adults leaves us asking ourselves questions. What do we care about so strongly about that we feel zealous towards? What motivates us each day to get up and go into the world to create something positive and meaningful? Do we act in a zestful manner to bring about that thing we care so deeply about? Where does living in a Santa Spirit framework fit into our lives? And could it be that living with an A-Z Santa Spirit has the potential to transform not just our lives but the lives of those for whom we care about most deeply?

Give it a try.

End Notes

29

End notes

[1] For detailed information on the history of Santa Claus, see Re-Imagine Santa by Yvonne Vissing (2020).

[2] Moore, Clement. (1988). The Night Before Christmas. New York: Putnam

[3] Church, Francis. (1897). Yes, Virginia there is a Santa. *New York Sun*

[4] Sullivan, Robert. (1996) *The Flight of the Reindeer*. MacMillian: NY.

[5] Piper, Watty. (2005). The *Little Engine That Could*. New York :Philomel Books : in association with Grosset & Dunlap

[6] Roosevelt, Eleanor. https://quoteinvestigator.com/2018/02/10/beauty-dreams/

[7] For more information, see Dr. Krznaric at the School of Life in London, his book Wonderbox: Curious Histories of How to Live or his articles at https://greatergood.berkeley.edu/profile/roman_krznaric

[8] Vissing, Yvonne. (2020). Re-Imagine Santa.

[9] Fulghum, Robert. (1988). *All I Ever Needed To Know I Learned In Kindergarten*. NewYork: Villard Books.

[10] Kongtrul, Dzigar. (2018). Training in Tenderness: Buddhist teachings on tsewa, the radical openness of heart that can change the world. Boston: Shambala.

[11] Old Farmer's Almanac. (2020). https://www.almanac.com/

[12] Bronners Christmas Wonderland. (2012). Ornament, Legends, Symbols and Traditions. www.bronners.com

[13] Polacco, Patricia. (1996). Trees of the Dancing Goats. NY: Simon and Schuster.

[14] Vissing, Yvonne. (2020). A Santa Spirit Advent Calendar Book.

[15] Vissing, Yvonne. (2020). The Legend of the Santa Stocking.

[16] Ranseth, Joseph. Nd. https://josephranseth.com/gandhi-didnt-say-be-the-change-you-want-to-see-in-the-world/

Cover photo

Santa sharing the spirit of loving-kindness. Shutterstock photo purchased with authorization to reproduce. Thank you to photographer-artist Sergey Nivens, 213737203

www.ingramcontent.com/pod-product-compliance
Lightning Source LLC
Chambersburg PA
CBHW030913080526
44589CB00010B/279